SECRETS *of* HEAVEN

OTHER NEW MESSAGE BOOKS

Steps to Knowledge

Greater Community Spirituality

Relationships & Higher Purpose

Living The Way of Knowledge

The New God

Life in the Universe

The Great Waves of Change

Wisdom from the Greater Community
Volumes I & II

The Allies of Humanity
Books I-III

A NEW MESSAGE BOOK

SECRETS of HEAVEN

mystery teachings of the angels

MARSHALL VIAN SUMMERS

SECRETS
OF
HEAVEN

Edited by Darlene Mitchell
Cover photo by Emiliano Ricci (flickr.com/photos/aeruginosa), licensed under CC BY 2.0

ISBN: 978-1-884238-16-1
Library of Congress Control Number: 2013913849

Publisher's Cataloging-in-Publication
(Provided by Quality Books, Inc.)

Summers, Marshall Vian.
Secrets of heaven: mystery teachings of the angels/
Marshall Vian Summers.
volumes cm
LCCN 2013913849
ISBN 9781884238161 (pbk.)
ISBN 9781884238901 (ebook)

1. Society for the New Message. 2. Spiritual life—
Society for the New Message. 3. Heaven--Miscellanea.
4. Angels--Miscellanea. 5. Spirit writings.
I. Title.
BP605.S58S835 2013 299'.93
QBI13-600126

The books of New Knowledge Library are published by The Society for the New Message. The Society is a religious non-profit organization dedicated to presenting and teaching a New Message for humanity.

The books of New Knowledge Library, of which *Secrets of Heaven* is one part, are being studied by people around the world in over 16 languages and can be ordered at newknowledgelibrary.org, amazon.com or your local bookstore.

To learn more about The Society's audio recordings, educational programs and contemplative services please visit newmessage.org or call 1-800-938-3891.

The Society for the New Message
P.O. Box 1724 Boulder, CO 80306-1724
(303) 938-8401 (800) 938-3891
011 303 938 84 01 (International) (303) 938-1214 (fax)
email: society@newmessage.org www.newknowledgelibrary.org
www.newmessage.org

♦ ♦ ♦

Dedicated to the mystery that

has brought you into the world

at this time and that holds

your greater purpose

for being here

SECRETS
OF
HEAVEN

table of contents

INTRODUCTION

WITHIN THESE PAGES IS THE BEGINNING of a direct communication from the heart of God to the heart of Creation in each of us. As you read, listen carefully. As you listen, you may feel the touch of your Ancient Home, the touch of your Spiritual Family and the touch of the Angelic Presence, that seeks to guide and protect you in your journey on Earth. Put away the burdens of your worldly mind and listen with your heart. It is time to enter the Mystery.

Secrets of Heaven represents the sacred engagement we are destined to have with God, the Angels of God and with Knowledge, the deeper spiritual intelligence within us. In the pages that follow, you can begin to experience this engagement for yourself.

This engagement is an environment of deep experience within you. It is here that you find you are no longer alone but are attended to by the Angelic Presence that has aided and guided you since the beginning of your time here on Earth. These are mysterious relationships to explore.

The engagement experience builds the foundation for receiving the guidance, direction and counsel you need to navigate your life in an increasingly uncertain world and to locate within the world the people, purpose and destiny that you must find. This inner engagement will yield the greatest discoveries of your life.

Secrets of Heaven was first revealed in 1983. Responding to the prayers of humanity, the Angelic Presence opened the source waters of Heaven's love and grace to flow into the world anew. In the most mysterious of circumstances, a man named

Marshall Vian Summers was called to be the recipient and Messenger for a New Revelation, of which *Secrets of Heaven* is but a small part. Since 1983, this gift from the Divine has not stopped. It continues to be revealed, coming to nourish and prepare us as we face new and perilous challenges in the world.

Each page of this book contains a secret from the Angelic Presence. Each secret offers a precious opportunity to open the doors of your perception and awareness. Now you can begin to see as Heaven sees. Now you are looking through the eyes of Heaven to see and experience yourself, others and the world as never before.

At the conclusion of this book is the seminal revelation "The Engagement," which takes you deeper into your mysterious connection with Knowledge and with those who sent you into the world.

Heaven asks you to receive its secrets. The Angels of Heaven seek to share their secrets with you. Through this book, these secrets are given to you now. May *Secrets of Heaven* be a doorway to a new life for you.

NEW KNOWLEDGE LIBRARY

SECRETS
of
HEAVEN

WE ARE ABOVE THE SURFACE OF YOUR WORLD, and yet your environment is as transparent to us as a shallow pond with fish. Even more so, since we have lived in that pond so many times ourselves. How much more we know. If the fish could but listen to the thoughts of its observers who stand over its domain, it could learn of everything else—of the trees and the sky, the flowers, the source of the water that feeds its pond and the destiny of the water that is drained from its pond. It is the same for you. You could learn what lies beyond your domain, for like the fish, you live within a whole universe, not within a little pond. Though the fish may live its entire life in such a small place, it swims in the whole universe, with the sky and the stars above it and below it as well. Is this not also true with you?

WE MAKE OURSELVES PUBLIC so that you may know our presence and know that there is a Master Plan. It is this Plan that you must now become aware of, for until you do, your life will be aimless, without certain purpose, with only your errors to teach you.

WE WISH FOR YOU ALL TO RECEIVE THE JOY that awaits you. In our world, there is joy. There are very few in this world who can contain the joy that we feel. We are not bound by what cannot succeed. We are not hopeless. We are not alone.

TO FOLLOW IS TO UNITE. To unite is to be reunited.

GOD MUST ENTER A WORLD where God is not welcome, in ways that do not generate fear and panic amongst those who believe the world is their only reality. It is for this reason that the Will of God manifests itself in subtle and ingenious ways in this world.

IN THE ABSENCE OF THE PRESENCE OF GOD, all questions arise. In the Presence of God, all questions disappear.

IN THIS WORLD THERE IS GREAT DEFERENCE given to freedom of choice, but to the elevated mind, choice is something to be escaped, not acquired.

BELIEFS HAVE A TEMPORARY SERVICE, to give you the framework in order to re-experience an experience that you have had already.

DO YOU THINK THAT THE PLAN CALLS for a bunch of dreamers? Ineffectual, impotent, lacking in courage? We assure you this is not the case. Strong you must be—gentle, sensitive and strong.

GOD ANSWERS THROUGH THE TEACHERS. They are God's answer. They can translate the Will of God into an experience that you can accept, recognize and appreciate. It is through these relationships that the Will of God will become ever present to you.

NOW THE OLD AGE DRAWS TO AN END. Difficult will its ending be and turbulent. And yet you are preparing for the advent of this change and the beginning of a new order. The turmoil that you have felt in your individual lives is an indication that you are in preparation for a world in change.

WHEN THE MIND IS JOINED WITH SPIRIT, it is in its true role. It recognizes its function and is capable of fulfilling it perfectly.

YOUR NEED TO RECEIVE IS GREAT INDEED. Accept your present limits. They are temporary, but you must work with them if you are to progress. Potentiality is not accomplishment. You are not masters. There are no masters living in this world, for mastery exists beyond this world.

IF YOU WILL BE A WITNESS TO YOUR FEAR, it will disappear. If you will be a witness to what is true, it will grow. It is this in your experience that will teach you the difference, and you will not have doubt.

REGARDING THE ISSUE OF LISTENING: many of you prepare to listen but give up too soon. The Teachers do not need preparation, but you need to find a way to hear, and this receptivity must be developed. It is retraining the mind to be in relationship.

THERE ARE MANY WONDERFUL DELAYS on your journey, but they are not wonderful because they are delays.

IN ORDER TO ENTER INTO HOLY UNION with your Teachers, you must share your Teachers' greatness, thus releasing you from the debilitating ideas and self-doubts that have been the context in which you have tried to organize and direct your affairs and establish your life in exile.

YOU CANNOT REACH GOD DIRECTLY without joining in holy relationships. Therefore, your interest in relationships is truly motivated, yet it is misinterpreted and misdirected. You feel the impulse, but you do not know where it comes from.

THE BODY, MADE AS A VEHICLE OF SEPARATION to hide and mask you, becomes holy as it is shared for a holy purpose.

YOU CAN DELAY, BUT YOU CANNOT CHANGE the path that you must choose. You may complain about the state of the world as you perceive it, but is it not merely a manifestation that your substitutes for happiness are failing you at last, and did you not unknowingly bring this about? Your state of separation is failing you, and you cannot escape this realization. Its miseries come to your attention every day.

RETREANA CARVEDAN CELTON IY. Receive the Heart of God through your Spiritual Family that is joined about you.

YOUR MANY REGRETS ARE THE THORNY CROWN that you wear. Remove it.

CLEAR THE WAY. Take courage. Without options, your way becomes clear.

THE WORLD WILL MOTIVATE YOU to find the truth for it offers you nothing.

IT IS TRUE INDEED that we have been assigned to you, out of our own choosing and yours as well. But you have forgotten and we have not.

YOU WILL LEARN TO SHARE YOUR BODY by recognizing the relationships that it contains. No longer will it be a prison house in which you think you live and die, but rather a temple where your loved ones come to join you in peace and matrimony.

IT IS TRUE THAT THE NETWORK OF TEACHERS is grand indeed. Great it is, beyond your imagination. It spans the entire universe, and all of the galaxies that have been created. For the Spiritual Families cannot be limited by time or space. Beyond all dimensions they reach, into the Heart of God. These are the Great Rays, for at the highest level, they become pure light, pure expression. And you will realize that you are not merely experiencing communication. You will realize you are communication. Your life is communication. Your Being is communication. There is nothing else.

WE CANNOT TAKE YOUR HABIT OF SUFFERING from you, but we can demonstrate to you that it is no longer of value to you, and need not be called upon in response to change or to new experience or information. You are still in charge of your experience, but you cannot lead yourself.

WE ASSURE YOU, YOU HAVE COME TO SEEK your Family. Whether you can accept this idea based on your previous beliefs is something that you must deal with at the outset, but we can assure you that you have come to seek your Family.

AT A CERTAIN STATE IN YOUR DEVELOPMENT, you will respond to those of your Spiritual Family, for they are kin to you in a way that you cannot describe. Deeply felt it is. You will know them. You will feel drawn. You will attempt to give reasons for your attraction, but you cannot, for it is a bond that runs deeper than your understanding. Stronger than your decisions it is.

THE WORLD CANNOT HEAL ITS ILLS. It knows not of its remedy. Nor will the world be perfected until what is beyond becomes acceptable. For a perfected world is like the gate that opens of itself. As long as the world is sought as a place of isolation, it will be maintained in chaos to serve that purpose.

GOD HAS WON THE WAR, but God's children keep fighting.

BE SATISFIED THAT YOU CAN FEEL OUR PRESENCE, for greater than words it is. Your heart will answer us. It knows the language that we speak, the mission that we share with you. For the heart is not blind and responds only to this one calling.

THE HOLY SPIRIT IS YOUR WILL. It is the will you share with God. It is the will you share with your Family. With it comes the Plan that will redeem you, establishing your special part, the part that only you can fulfill. What God gave you is your will, for God gave you Knowledge.

AS YOUR FAMILY MEMBERS GATHER WITHIN YOU and about you, they render to you all that they have learned.

THE MERE FACT THAT YOU BELIEVE YOU HAVE CHOICES is an indication that your certainty is beyond your awareness. For when you know, there is no choice. What is known is of God. In time, your Knowing will become so strong that the burden of decision making will fall away from you. Without choices, the mind is free and can rest and enjoy, unafraid of what it must choose between. Without choice is perfect faith in the knowledge that everything that is known leads to greater peace.

IT TAKES FAR LONGER TO PREPARE than it does to act.

AS YOU BECOME RECEPTIVE, you will hear many voices. Not all of them will speak truly. Become a good listener.

THE WORLD WILL NEED YOU, and you must commit yourself to it. It is not a world of casual choices but a world of great demands, and the demands that it will make will show you your own greatness.

WHEN YOU SPEAK THE TRUTH, everyone benefits, and yet the truth you speak cannot be verified by your questioning mind, for it does not come from this source.

THE WILL OF GOD IS CONSIDERED AN OPTION and not a certainty. As long as this be the case, we must instruct you in how to choose wisely. But beyond this, choosing is not necessary.

THE TEACHERS WILL GIVE YOU A PURE EXPERIENCE of relationship. You cannot see them; they are hard to judge. Your affinity for them will be firmly established before their appearance becomes known.

WHENEVER THE PRESENCE OF LOVE IS FELT, it is always the result of a relationship being experienced, whether it be a relationship of which you are aware or unaware. This Presence is merely the product of relationship.

THE EXPERIENCE OF GOD DIRECTLY is the experience of all relationships at once.

WE HAVE SPOKEN MANY TIMES about the experience of God in the context of relationship and communication. It is brought to you in this way so that you may practice with everything with which you come into contact.

DO YOU KNOW WHENEVER YOU ARE UPSET or afraid, it is always because you think you are alone? It is not possible to be upset or afraid if you are not alone. Indeed, the value of knowing one other is with you is enough to inspire you to do great works within your world. Only one. And yet you have thousands.

WE HAVE INTRODUCED THE IDEA of Spiritual Families to broaden your horizon for relationship, which is your ability to communicate and to integrate more and more of God's Creation within your mental thought system. For family is primary to your experience of relationship. And yet how much greater is the Spiritual Family to which you will be called for the deepening of your experience.

WE KNOW HOW TO RESOLVE THE DIFFICULTIES that the world faces because we have resolved them for ourselves.

THERE IS NO PRIVACY. And yet, truly, this is your salvation because all that you desire is with you. Ones that you have loved in lives past, the accomplishments you have made, the dear ones with whom you have bonded, are all available to you now.

IF THE MIND IS NOT PREOCCUPIED with its own thoughts, it naturally gives and receives communication. In fact, it does this even when it is preoccupied, but it is not aware that this is occurring.

WE REPRESENT A GOOD MODEL FOR RELATIONSHIP because we cannot be seen unless we wish to. And yet our Presence is so deeply felt by those who allow us to enter their consciousness. If you were to pass from your body this evening, you would simply awaken in our presence.

YOU MUST ALWAYS SEARCH YOURSELF, for we may tell you things to challenge you. We wish to stimulate your thinking, not replace it.

THE WORLD WILL RARELY AGREE WITH YOU. However, you possess something that everyone knows. It is an opportunity to overlook what is of little value and to emphasize what really matters.

THE DESCENT INTO THE WORLD necessitates a loss of vision, a loss of communication. It is the nature of the world which requires that this be so.

YOUR LITTLE WORLD, SEEMINGLY SO ISOLATED and so far from life, a little ball floating through the darkness, is surrounded by a vast array of developments and civilizations, both within and beyond your perceptual range.

THERE IS A GREAT EMPHASIS PLACED ON THOSE who respond to an inner calling. They have such importance. We gather around them. They hold the promise of renewal and rejuvenation for your world.

WE ONLY SEEK TO TEACH WHAT IS NATURAL to you and to your needs. When you are not in your body, on the next plane, so many things are obvious to you. Your desire to return and remedy your situation is great indeed. It is for this reason that you wish to return here. And yet until that initial purpose is re-established in your consciousness, you are lost—survival being your predominant interest, self-protection your most important concern.

LEARNING TO COMMUNICATE, you recognize your reluctance to do so and your habit of self-absorption—of entertaining your own thoughts rather than discovering what is true. This attempt to be alone has produced suffering and nothing else.

WHEN YOU ARE NOT IN A PHYSICAL BODY, you are between levels. Here you have a greater awareness of what is possible. But you cannot participate fully.

YOUR ONLY INTEREST IS IN RELATIONSHIP. You may believe from your unhappy experiences in attempting communication with others that it is not worth the effort. However, you will never give up.

FOR YOUR OWN LEARNING PROGRESS, you are joined with certain leagues of beings. Think not that their establishment is limited to the associations of nations and races of peoples. This establishment pervades and includes all worlds such as yours, of which there are many thousands, we assure you.

ALL FAMILIES CONVERGE IN ONE FAMILY. And yet, until this occurs, you will have specific callings to specific people. You will have specific courses of action to take with specific people. You have been assigned specific Teachers. You do not have the ability to dismiss them.

FOR MANY, JESUS IS THE SYMBOL and the guiding factor in their development. But let us assure you that he is not the only one. A greater association there is, lest you make of him an idol, an object, which he does not will.

WE MUST WATCH OUR WORDS VERY CAREFULLY. Do you see, you are so prone to predictions and those things that are sensational. We do not wish to speak of such things. Misused they are. It is difficult to use a piece of specific information in a constructive way, particularly when it concerns the future. Your future world is contingent upon you and upon others as well. It cannot be understood based upon your own life path alone.

THINK NOT THERE WILL BE AN END TO LEARNING after you have left the world. This world is only a beginning.

IN ORDER TO PROTECT YOU in your learning and assure that you progress, we have remained hidden.

MY TEACHER SPOKE OF THESE THINGS TO ME over eighteen thousand years ago. I did not believe him. He came again and again. I would not listen. It seemed irrelevant. The times were difficult. The old empire had passed. Civilization was scattered and lost, and many great ones were driven underground and destroyed. Pursued they were. Records of history were destroyed. It was a period of great undoing. In the face of such calamities, the words he spoke seemed barely relevant to me. And yet I chose to listen, for I had heard his words before. An ancient chord was struck in me, an ancient memory. I had a recall of an experience before birth that I could not forget. They placed me on a dais and prepared me to enter the world. They cast a light over my head and they said, "You will not forget this light." And I remembered. My Teacher, who is with me now as he was then, prepared me. Things that you encounter are far less difficult though you have many more needs and complexities in your life than we did. Food and shelter—these were our concerns. You have many concerns we did not even dream of.

BEING WITHIN A BODY IN THE WORLD necessitates a certain level of ignorance. Accept this. Do not strive for total awareness, or you will neglect what can actually be done here.

MY TEACHER, ANCIENT HE IS. He does not exist on my level now. He speaks to me purely through thought. Our thoughts are shared. This is how I know him. He has ceased to be a separate individual. And yet he is easily recognizable. His thoughts are far too refined for you. They would pass through your mind as if it were not there.

WE ARE VERY CAREFUL. There is already much controversy and philosophy concerning Master Teachers and much partial evidence. Yet we assure you that the nature and the organization of the Teachers is beyond your capability to appreciate.

THE TRAGEDIES THAT YOU PERCEIVE within your world are minor. All they do is destroy the communication process. The purpose of attack is nothing other than to disable communication.

YOUR WORK NOW IS WITHIN THE WORLD. You cannot leave here until your work is done. If you destroy your learning vehicle, you will simply have to wait and return again. Indeed, you will be anxious to return, for as you wait, you will recognize the opportunities that you missed. Recognizing your errors, you will be anxious to return.

CHILDREN DREAM OF BEING ADULTS, but they must still be children to grow.

WE HOLD THE KEY, but you possess the treasure. We cannot contribute without you, and you cannot contribute without us. It is a good Plan.

MANY OF YOU ARE EXPERIENCING GREAT CHANGE. We know this. It is not an easy task. But you cannot return to your previous securities, for you have seen them to be lacking to your need. You must press forward.

TELL US, WHAT DO YOU KNOW? You see, if we answer your question, you will say, "My Teachers said this, and my Teachers said that, and my Teachers told me to do this, and I don't want to." And then it will be your Teachers' problem. What do you know?

YOU ARE ALL MEMBERS OF A SPIRITUAL FAMILY. Over this you have no control. The revelation of this will come in time, though perhaps not within your own lifetime, unless it is important for you to recognize. When you leave this world, you will regroup with those who have been attending to you, as well as with those who have entered the world with you to learn in parallel with you. Perhaps many of them you will never meet in the world. Some of them you will. You have been working with this group for some time. That is why there is such great recognition amongst those who share your group cooperation. Your group interacts with other groups as well. The complexity of this you cannot imagine. Yet it operates according to natural law without deviation. Your Family group has a name because at this level, names are significant to you. Beyond this level, they have sounds or frequencies.

THE SPIRITUAL FAMILIES WERE ESTABLISHED before the physical universe existed. They were established as a plan of union, organizing all separated beings into a learning procedure that would accurately serve them in their individual needs, while organizing them into learning groups that would aspire to greater and greater levels of understanding. These levels would transcend all of the physical planes into the etheric and beyond. The Family establishment was according to the great Plan, for indeed, there is a great Plan.

THE ONLY PURPOSE OF INTRODUCING THIS IDEA of Spiritual Families at this time is to prepare you for contact with life beyond the world. Within the Earth, this means little. And yet the Earth is part of a Greater Community.

AT THIS TIME, AS YOUR COMMITMENT to participate will grow, your wisdom must grow as well. This is not an easy task. For you must wholeheartedly participate in something that you cannot understand and perhaps only rarely experience.

ALL OF THESE IDEAS MUST BE PURIFIED AND CLEANSED of older associations you have had with them, for there is great distrust. This we recognize.

SECRETS
OF
HEAVEN

♦

TO STUDENTS OF KNOWLEDGE WHO ARE LEARNING to accept our Presence, we honor your being here. Again, we recognize the difficulties involved. It is a transition from one level of thought to another. The levels have little to do with one another, and to reach one that is higher, you must abandon the former. The in-between transition stages can be very confusing. And yet what motivates you is beyond your control, and this is the power that you seek.

KNOWLEDGE BRINGS RESPONSIBILITY, and purpose always has a calling. Indeed, the function of purpose is the response to a calling. You cannot understand your purpose without acting upon it. This action will call for perhaps a greater participation and understanding than you have ever known.

WHEN YOU KNOW, YOU KNOW. And your choice is made already. It is this experience that you will want to seek out in your decision making at this point. Decisions made without this are merely presumptions. They may have great emotion, but they do not have a foundation. Those who have purpose are not burdened with decisions.

YOU LEARN TO BE IN RELATIONSHIP with the Teachers who are assigned to develop your skills and to reveal your purpose. It will be far easier for them, for they are not deceived or confused. A greater assistance you cannot imagine. And yet to enter into this relationship is to assign yourself to your purpose and its calling. You cannot use your purpose for yourself, for the mind cannot use the Spirit.

WHAT GOD HAS GIVEN YOU is complete relationship and a higher purpose. These will be seen as burdens until they are recognized as the means to regain your freedom.

OF COURSE OUR WORDS CANNOT EXPRESS the essence of the Teaching that we relate to you. This must always happen in the very deepest part of you. And yet our words bring with them a memory.

IT IS ESSENTIAL THAT THE WORLD UNDERGO its transition into the Greater Community. It is the end of childhood, and with it many things will pass. Do not be concerned with complete destruction, for that is not the way of things. Be concerned instead with supporting the world through this state of transition.

IT IS FOR YOUR PROTECTION that the Plan is completely beyond your control. You cannot govern it, change it or turn it to serve your own designs. Hardly possible. It is therefore safe and for your protection.

WHAT ESTABLISHES COMMUNITY is never the charisma of a leader. It is the Presence of that which guides the leader. This is true community. It is this that you must learn and teach.

DEVELOPMENT IN THE INDIVIDUAL is always the ability to participate in relationship. If you will think of your own advancement in this way, you will recognize your true path. There have been many who have been turned away because they have failed to see this. Though their practices gave them great insight, they were not able to join the Greater Community, for they had not developed this ability.

INDEED, THE RECOGNITION OF THE HIERARCHY assigns all power and authority beyond any society. In order for a society to allow this and give it license, it must have developed into a higher state. This world does not afford this luxury, and there are few that do. When this occurs, the world may actually refine its manifest expression and move into another dimension. There are worlds that have literally disappeared from the view of those who remain behind.

AND SO WE HAVE THE PARADOX OF WORDS. How can you exist as an individual but not be an individual? How can you have total freedom and no choice? These things cannot be understood here. Indeed, they may incite fear and misinterpretation. It is for this reason that the Greater Plan establishes in each world its own educational process, depending upon the nature of that world's customs, the make-up of its societies and its own dilemmas.

THERE ARE MANY TEACHERS WHO SERVE this world, for this is the world of their lineage. There are Teachers of those Teachers who serve the Greater Community at large, and there are Teachers of those Teachers, and so on and so forth. You are not asked to understand this, for you could not be in the world and have this understanding. But you are all asked to receive those who have been sent to help and guide you.

YOU THINK YOUR ENLIGHTENMENT OCCURS within you alone. All progress is the result of relationship. Your enlightenment is the recognition of complete relationship.

THE TEACHERS DO NOT KNOW EVERYTHING, yet they possess the Wisdom that you must seek and accomplish. They are guided as well. In this way, there is no one who is not attended to, for everyone belongs.

IT WOULD BE WISE INDEED TO RELINQUISH the idea of personal enlightenment altogether. It is a misnomer. The person you are seeking to enlighten is the obstacle that stands in your way. Who you are is not the person you seek to enlighten.

ANY ATTEMPT TO USE YOUR RELATIONSHIP with the Teachers to satisfy your personal ends is of no concern to them. They acknowledge their purpose and nothing else. And since they do not have personal ends, they cannot corrupt the bond that you establish with them.

IF YOU HAVE PURPOSE, you will teach it. If you do not have purpose, you must seek it.

EVERYONE WANTS TO KNOW THE ANSWER without making the journey. It is the journey that is the answer.

WHAT YOU CALL YOUR HIGHER SELF is your Self in relationship. Let us make this important distinction, lest your isolation become sanctified: that which you call your Higher Self is yourself in relationship unended.

THOSE WHO HAVE GREAT PURPOSE follow their individual role without attempting to follow any other. And yet they become less and less individual. As they become less individual, they become more relationship. For who you are is relationship.

THEREFORE, YOU MUST ENTER RELATIONSHIP with purpose to learn of purpose. As you have entered relationships for folly, you have learned of folly; as you have entered relationships of pain, you have learned of pain. You must recognize pain as pain or you will continue to seek it as pleasure. Unfortunately, this may take a great deal of time. But fortunately for you, you do not have this kind of time. The demands of your world are requiring that you lay aside learning at your own pace. You must now learn at the pace that is required.

THERE IS IMPATIENCE AMONGST YOU, and yet we assure you that your first step will seem like too much.

THERE IS GREAT EMPHASIS IN THE WORLD on developing individual control and self-assertion. This is valuable only insofar as it gives you the strength and the discipline to be strong enough to relinquish all self-assertion.

IT IS THE STATE THAT JESUS ACQUIRED that you most earnestly desire. You must not then make a hero of him, or you will lose what he has accomplished. Regarding the religion that has been established around him, it has little to do with him, we assure you. It offers the promise of his accomplishment, though it does not establish the means.

YOU WHO ARE WORRIED ABOUT THE PURITY of your intentions must test them in action to discover the outcome. Those who seek purity first will not participate. The participation itself will establish the ability to respond and to receive. All purification means is relinquishing the obstacles to participation. The personal illusions and dilemmas must be burned away so that a person may be able to join in relationship with true purpose. Therefore, concern yourself not with purity, for you will disable yourself. You cannot establish purity when you are not sure what it is. Instead, allow yourself to follow what you know to be true and do not hesitate. You will find this a great enough challenge.

YOUR MIND IS SO TIRED OF ORGANIZING and collecting information that you have no time for relationship. It is odd because relationship provides all the necessary information.

IT IS NOT THOSE FROM AFAR in the Greater Community who will save you, for they share your same difficulties and obstacles. It is your hope that they are all very enlightened, yet this is not true. Amongst them there are as many great ones as there are here. Their skills vary as well as their technological development. Their range of communication and association vary as well. Yet Wisdom is Wisdom in whatever land and culture, in whatever environment and within whatever creature it may touch.

WHAT IS FALSE MUST FAIL. When what is false has failed you, you will then appreciate the assistance that has been given you. Then help will not seem to be a contrivance; it will not seem to be an interference. It will not be seen as a sacrifice, but as the true assistance that it is.

HAVE YOU NOT WONDERED, being as intelligent as you seem to be, why you have not been able to resolve your dilemmas? Indeed, many of you establish relationships and involvements fully knowing that they will not prosper and progress. And yet you will maintain them with great devotion. Why is this? Is it not curious? It is because you seek to establish a condition for choosing that will be unequivocal.

UNTIL YOU HAVE REACHED A STATE OF NO-CHOICE, you have not landed on solid ground. It is this condition of no-choice that fosters decision making with importance. Think not that you understand this until you have experienced it.

DO NOT BECOME A PERFECT INDIVIDUAL, for you will be nothing, though greatly praised within the world. A very valuable nothing.

YOUR HIGHER SELF IS NOT AN INDIVIDUAL. It is but a relationship. This is what makes it higher. There are no higher individuals, but there are great relationships.

THOSE WHO SEEK FREEDOM must relinquish freedom entirely. There is no freedom in freedom. It is when you move out of freedom that you are free. Is this not a contradiction? When there is choice, there is bondage, for you have not reached what is irrevocable. Only what is irrevocable has freedom, for only it is consistent and whole and at peace, because it is irrevocable. An irrevocable decision is not a decision. It is Knowledge.

IF WE BUT GIVE YOU THE FIRST PIECE OF THE PUZZLE, will you run around saying it is the answer, when it is but the first piece? And can you wait patiently while hundreds of pieces are given to you, patiently fitting them together in sequence?

EVEN FOR A MOMENT TRY TO FEEL THE GATHERING that occurs in truth about you—this is called the crown, a gathering of servants. It is as if your mind were but a fire, and they gather about to watch its flames. Into the fire they give their counsel and their love to you.

WITHIN THE WORLD, ALL PEOPLE ARE CONVERGING. It is the end of tribal structure. It is the end of separate states. And resisted this is. All of the grievances that have existed for thousands of years are now becoming felt and sharply manifested. Is this convergence not given great support by those who wait to reunite with others who share their lineage here? And is the world not observed by those of good virtue and by those of no virtue?

INDEED, YOU HAVE LITTLE NOTION of what exists
beyond your boundaries. The world is like a village
that has never been touched by the outside world.
Preoccupied it is with its own difficulties and concerns.
People in the village are very concerned, but ignorant.
And as the outside world encroaches upon this village,
does it not begin to feel the stress of this? And do not
its divisions become manifested as it looks outward?
It is a fair analogy. This world is a tiny village, preoccupied
with itself, as when you were a tiny child preoccupied with
yourself. And was not growing into adulthood difficult,
with many disappointments and times of stress? And did
not your parents look upon you, in wisdom perhaps,
and remark that it was a difficult age to pass through
as you became part of something greater, responsible
for something greater and accountable to something greater?

OUR NAMES ARE NOT KNOWN IN THE WORLD. It is because our charge is not this world alone. There are many Teachers who attend to the world singularly. It is their purpose to do so. And yet our charge is to unite this world and prepare it for the Greater Community.

THE WORLD IS OPENING. Opening is difficult. It takes great planning and support, as well as great willingness. The factions that are intent upon maintaining tribal separation will struggle against this as if it were their own identity that they were seeking to save. And yet this must pass as well. To understand your visitors from beyond the world, you must be beyond divisiveness among yourselves. This is a lofty goal, given your present state. And yet the forewarning of this is but the symbol of the purpose that underlies change as you know it. Do not think that this will not involve you completely. You have no greater desire than to become completely involved. For in this way, you will become complete.

YOU ARE TERRIFIED OF INVOLVEMENT for fear of sacrifice, for fear of what you might have to give up. Actually, you are afraid that you would be happy to give up everything for total involvement. The truth that you are afraid of is your own will. For, in coming in contact with your own will, all else becomes irrelevant. Nothing else concerns you.

IT IS THE PLAN NOT OF YOUR MAKING that will rescue you from the dilemma that has no resolution.

IT IS NOT OUR PURPOSE to give you mightier options, but to re-establish your ability to regain Knowledge, and with Knowledge, relationship.

THOSE WHO RESPOND TO US are given tasks which utilize them so greatly. For in this way, they recognize their greatness. How may greatness be recognized save by its application?

BE PREPARED, THEN, FOR THE VISITATION of those from the Greater Community. Yet you must be counseled. They are not all of good intention. A young adolescent entering the world of adults will discover the world through exposure. Many ideals and hopes perhaps will be lost encountering the real nature and state of those who are met. Thus it is with the emergence of this world into the Greater Community. Why is this relevant to you? It is relevant because it represents the time in history during which you have entered the world. It is your responsibility to serve this history, fulfilling your rightful place and thus completing your mission here.

CONTACT WITH THE TEACHERS is an exercise in remembering your true mind and your true relationships. The purpose inherent in this is to call you into service.

YOU ARE GUARDIANS OF A TREASURE UNKNOWINGLY. Your treasure is your lineage, the accrued learning of all of your activities here and abroad.

YOU ARE ALL PREOCCUPIED WITH YOURSELVES. It is because you have learned to do this. And yet you will need to become preoccupied with what is beyond yourself. This is your salvation, we assure you.

YOU CANNOT CHANGE YOUR GREATER PURPOSE nor alter it to serve any other purpose. It is its inherent purity that establishes it as the saving grace within yourself. It represents the part of your mind that is beyond the world, yet which seeks to serve and fulfill its purpose even here.

THE PREOCCUPATION WITH ERROR is nothing more than a decision not to know.

MANY OF YOU WILL ASK, "WHAT IS MY PURPOSE?" Your purpose is to discover your Knowledge and to serve God and God's Hierarchy.

MANY OF YOU WILL WONDER who we are. We are what you will become.

YOUR LIFE HAS TWO POSSIBILITIES. You will find your purpose and fulfill it, or you will not. It is only your success in this matter that you will reflect upon once you leave. For upon leaving the world, you will leave all the world's preoccupations, leaving you with your one purpose, fulfilled or not.

YOU WILL SEE IN THE DAYS TO COME Knowledge and belief and the great contrast between them. What is known has no boundaries. What is believed sets them.

PREFERENCES ARE ESTABLISHED in the absence of Knowledge. They are mindless and destructive, for they betray your basic instincts and greater tendencies.

TO BE SET ON THE PATH OF GOOD does not always look good. To learn of God does not always seem holy. To learn of Wisdom is certainly beyond human logic.

ALL THAT WE SPEAK OF is the inherent process of discovering what is true by eliminating the false. First, you discover what is true by recognizing the contrast, for this contrast will teach you the source of your happiness and of your sorrow. Once this recognition has been developed, you may actually make a valuable decision, recognizing the source of happiness and the source of sorrow. This does not mean that happiness will become altogether desirable, yet your preferences will move more towards that which gives you a sense of wholeness.

PEOPLE HAVE GREAT ATTACHMENT TO THEIR ANGER. It is very significant to them. Yet it is rarely an indicator of what they know. Indeed, anger is the result of denying what is known. This is what produces anger in all cases.

SEARCH YOUR MIND in those issues which are most relevant to you and determine your preferences and beliefs in contrast to what you know. You may then ask the Teachers to help you find what you know and thus begin a useful and cooperative venture together.

IF YOU WERE GIVEN YOUR TRUE DESIRE IMMEDIATELY, your personality would be shattered. You would become dysfunctional and would perish. Not because your gift is destructive, but because you have no capacity for containing it.

MANY HAVE ATTEMPTED TO REACH GOD according to their own concepts and have become estranged from life as a result.

THE REASON YOUR MIND IS SO BEYOND your capacity to understand is because it contains Knowledge that has direct bearing on the lives of others. Much of this remains hidden, beyond your reach. Seek not to try to find it on your own accord, or there will be much damage, we assure you. The reclamation of spiritual powers is a very serious matter, one that has grave consequences if you err on its behalf. It is for this reason that when people ask how to regain power and purpose, for they are the same, we always speak of a procedure. You cannot jump ahead of where you are, and you must establish a firm foundation if you are to proceed wisely.

IF YOU ASPIRE TO REGAIN KNOWLEDGE, then you will in time reclaim your mission in the world as well, which is quite specific and well defined. It is not something that you can establish on your own accord, for it was merely given to you before your arrival in this place. If you are to claim this, then you must be prepared to be a person of great character and tremendous inner strength and honesty. There can be no self-deception in your mind, for it will play great havoc in your development and indeed will lead you astray.

YOUR LEARNING PREDICAMENTS HERE are the same as they are everywhere. You must be sensible in this matter, for you see, your world will be visited in very visible ways by races in the Greater Community, and you will be all excited because you may think it is the arrival of enlightened ones who possess great technological advancements that will free your people. Do not be foolish.

THE DIFFICULTY FOR YOU, indeed, is that your Knowledge is not based upon your personal wishes at all. You cannot alter it to serve your goals, most of which were created out of ignorance. Without Knowledge, you will merely create the substitutes under which you now live predominantly. What must be discovered through experience is that these wishes are the obstacles to your happiness and fulfillment. We emphasize Knowledge because it is the solid ground upon which you can make wise decisions. The Teachers will cultivate this skill within you. For if you relate to another who is honest and truly holds your best interests firmly in mind, you will become honest yourself. All forms of deception will become recognized, and the opportunity for correction will be presented to you.

YOUR WORLD IS IN A PREDICTABLE STAGE of evolution. Think not it is unique, for all civilizations pass through these difficult transition periods. Many of them fail. Humanity is in the process of entering a more mature state.

YOUR LEARNING, IF YOU CHOOSE TO PURSUE IT honestly, will be seemingly uncomfortable on many occasions. There seems to be universal agreement on that point. However, we will lessen the difficulties as much as possible. Yet your propensity to suffer and to examine yourself critically is not something that we can control. It is of great concern in the preparation of students, for they will see their errors as a weakness on their part. Often these errors are strengths in disguise. Yet the justification for these errors will not be of any service.

YOU MUST LEARN OF YOUR WEAKNESSES—all of them. Indeed, to discover any of them too late would be tragic.

YOU MUST SERVE A PLAN that is beyond your control. The amazing feature is that you will need to establish perfect control of yourself to be able to follow it.

YOU WILL KNOW US because we are your Family. This can only be known and is not realized through deduction or any kind of rational process. An old friend is merely recognized. If you remember us as we truly are, you will remember your life before entering here. You will remember your purpose and your agreement. You will remember the strength of your undertaking and the great assistance that surrounds you always. In this, you will find true strength, for nothing that you can see in the world can cast shadows upon an awareness of this magnitude.

YOU MUST BECOME ONE PERSON with one goal and one reference within yourself. This is the nature of healing. Healing is not merely the reparation of bodily functions or the calming of emotional disturbances. As long as your mind is divided, you are sick and in need of healing, regardless of any procedure that you may choose on your own behalf.

THERE WILL ALWAYS BE THOSE who will seek to misuse you if you offer services to them. You must be aware of them, both in the flesh and beyond. In this, your Knowledge is your protection, for it recognizes only those who speak for the truth around and within you. And yet to learn this discernment, you must become honest beyond your current definitions. You must not protect anything that betrays your Knowledge. And you must distinguish your Knowledge from your convictions and cherished ideals. A difficult task, yet one which you are given time and right circumstances to bring into fruition.

IF YOU ARE TO RECALL YOUR LINEAGE and with it the knowledge of your mission here, you must be able to expand beyond your human identity and affairs and yet bring all that you discover back to serve them.

OUR ADVICE YOU WILL DISREGARD UNDER PRESSURE. But your Knowledge you cannot disregard. It is wiser then to give you Knowledge than advice. You can only remember us through your Knowledge. Otherwise, we are just a phenomenon. You will forget everything we have said.

YOU ARE AFRAID OF WHAT YOU KNOW, for it will change your life utterly and offer you a true possibility for happiness, which is at present remote. Until then, you will merely attempt things until you find out that they fail you.

AS YOUR MIND BECOMES MORE EXPANSIVE, you will begin to experience a broad range of things—presences, communications and so forth. Yet this does not denote wisdom.

YOUR HEART WILL DIRECT YOU. It is this we have spoken of before. Listen to your heart. It is not your emotions that we speak of, but your Knowledge.

UNLESS YOU FEEL WHAT YOU KNOW, your feelings are of little value and are transitory, being merely reactions within themselves.

THE SPIRITUAL FAMILIES SERVE ALL WORLDS. Yet there are very few individuals within any world who are aware of the Families. Only those worlds that are culturally advanced and unified can have the knowledge of the Families amongst their populace.

WHAT WOULD IT AVAIL YOU TO KNOW OF US unless your participation was requested?

YOUR WORLD HAS MADE IT POSSIBLE for many of you to now seek greater things without hindrance. The temporary freedoms you experience in your world bear witness to this fact.

YOU WILL NEED STRONG ALLIES. Think not that you can prepare yourself. It has never been done. Anywhere. So do not think you are the exception to the entire universe.

YOU WILL ALWAYS KNOW THE OUTCOME of a relationship if you choose to listen.

WE GIVE PERSONAL RELATIONSHIPS the greatest priority, for they have the greatest potential for strengthening or weakening those who participate.

WE WISH TO CULTIVATE YOUR KNOWLEDGE so that you may make wise decisions. You need to do this particularly for those who follow you. If you are to teach the restoration of Knowledge within the world, which is your purpose, then you must learn to reclaim it for yourself in the areas of greatest personal preference.

IT IS NOT SO IMPORTANT that there are differences in the Spiritual Families. What is important is that you are a part of one. The differences really exist beyond the human level completely. The Families are merely separated to serve divergent interests and viewpoints. Their methods are unique. Yet they complement the needs of those who are their members.

THIS IDEA OF THE SPIRITUAL FAMILIES will be received with a mixture of responses. It is hoped that all are one in God, and yet we all learn through groups and procedures. Do you see, the Master Plan has taken all of your developments—personal relationships, marriage, children, groups, religion, government, everything—and given them a new function and purpose. God is very smart. God will win at your own game. It is not an easy task to win at your game. Only the Master Mind can think of this. God will use the divisions of separation to unite the entire universe.

IT IS NOT IMPORTANT WHETHER YOU BELIEVE in our presence or not. This can only be known, and belief adds little testimony to it.

YOUR FOCUS CANNOT BE ON THIS WORLD ALONE, for this world is not alone. Ultimately, its fate rests in the hands of the Spiritual Families.

THE VALUES OF THIS WORLD will be so affected by your emergence into the Greater Community. There has never been an impact so great upon the consciousness of those who dwell here nor one of such grave consequences. Religion, art, philosophy, culture, the foundations of government, law and ethics—all will be greatly affected.

THOSE WHO CLING TO THE OLD struggle against the forces of change, which seem to undermine all that they hold dear. Therefore, be cognizant of the value that the past has preserved and open to a future of very different proportions, while keeping in mind that all change, all phenomena and all beings, regardless of form or orientation, are part of the same learning procedure towards God.

THE EVENTS TO COME will require a shift in reality of the Earth's inhabitants. They must change or struggle against what they now experience. It is but this alone that they anticipate in their attempts to revive the old religions, systems and values, many of which have served a valuable purpose, yet in essence are long past. Are not the preparations of this century with its revivals, its new understandings, its outbreaks of conflict and its technological development but a preparation for what lies beyond in the new centuries to come? Has not all of this been building so rapidly towards a major turning point, as if racing to a finish that is in itself but a new beginning?

YOU ARE THE KNOWLEDGE THAT WE SPEAK OF. You do not merely possess or reclaim Knowledge. It is not a possession. It is not an acquisition. It is not a bestowal. You must become the force that joins all life, rather than one of its constituents alone.

IT IS NOT ENOUGH TO ACCEPT A NEW IDENTITY as more preferable, for you have been many places in your travels and yet your destiny, like those who follow you, is to become the bond and not the bonded. Can this be understood except through profound experience? No, it cannot.

YOU WILL BECOME neither God nor God's creation, but the relationship between the two. Reality is relationship. It is neither the individual nor the whole, as you think of these things.

SO MANY TESTIMONIES HAVE BEEN MADE to the infinite, to the gods, to the power of love and brotherhood, and yet only those who are this power can generate a true change with lasting effect.

HAVE FAITH THAT YOUR HEART KNOWS THE WAY to its Home, for without interference, it will simply travel its natural and inevitable course back to its Home, back to its true relationships, yet seemingly forward, far forward beyond all that you have experienced thus far.

INNER KNOWLEDGE, TRUE PURPOSE, the presence of the Teachers—all sound an inner calling that must grow in strength and scope as it is attended to and utilized, recognized and applied. All that is in contradiction to this at some point will be recognized and relinquished as unwanted, as merely hindering that natural return of the heart.

WE WILL NOT DEPRIVE YOU, though we may ask you for periods of time to limit your involvements so that you may have a new perception and a greater experience of yourself and of the world in which you live. These are temporary expedients. They offer opportunity, for new opportunities can only arise under special conditions.

WE RECOMMEND THAT YOU NOT JUDGE OTHERS in the world. Recognize that when this is done, your mind is closed. Perceive their predicament if you can, yet judge them not, nor their place, for they are on the path of choosing, one and all.

WHEN YOU WISH TO CONTACT US, simply allow your thoughts to settle, or pass through them as if they were nothing but wisps of vapor within a fog. For what is the fog but your own thoughts? These thoughts are not your real thoughts, for your real thoughts emanate from that part of yourself of which we speak, being the greater immortal aspect of you.

THOUGH MUCH OF WHAT WE HAVE TO SAY represents a profound wisdom and a practical application within your world, our desire to impart information to you is but the welcome mat we lay before you to enter into this greater communion.

IT IS BECAUSE YOU DRAW from your Greater Reality that you may establish something of greatness in the world, for nothing in the world is great.

YOU WILL SEE THROUGH YOUR OWN EXPERIENCE that no matter how miserable an individual's life may be, his or her misery is really a protection against the Greater Reality of which we speak. With this awareness, you will learn true compassion and will not be impatient with those who seem to progress slowly or not at all. Though you may offer them hope of release from their own bondage, you must recognize that they are afraid of this release as well.

THE EXPERIENCE OF GREATNESS will give you the perspective needed to give yourself permission to follow what you know.

YOUR DUTIES ARE OPPORTUNITIES to turn all that you have made into that which is good. Thus, everything that is here becomes a vehicle and a means for establishing true communication and relationship in a world of separate lives and empty hopes. Think on these things, yet do not make conclusions, for you will fall short if you do so.

YOU MUST, IN A SENSE, SUSPEND YOUR IDEA OF FAMILY, for even this word we choose only because it is familiar. It would be wiser to say it is an order of learning, an area of participation in the Greater Plan.

YOU CANNOT CHOOSE WHOLENESS from separation, but you can choose a greater participation that will make wholeness available to you within your realm of experience.

INDEED, THE DEFINITIONS OF THE JOURNEY that your world possesses are singularly lacking, for they do not
hold in scope the greater creation, even of manifest reality,
not to mention the greater realms that are not manifest.

WHAT IS YOUR SPIRITUAL FAMILY then but an experience of your foundation, given within a framework that you can cherish and accept? God has established a Plan that works because it reorders all levels of separation into a functioning and moving organization. It includes everyone. It is far more masterful of your creations than you are.

YOU CANNOT FIND TRUTH ALONE, for the truth is you are not alone.

IT IS THE TENDENCY WITHIN THIS WORLD—and indeed within all worlds—to identify with a concept or a belief, to identify with a thought system, instead of preparing yourself for a direct experience. Indeed, some thought systems claim that this is their goal. Yet the experience must come first. If the experience does not come first, the thought system will be the goal and not the means towards attaining something greater. Therefore, do not even have a concept of Spiritual Family. It is merely terminology we use because it is relevant to your experience here. Spiritual Family is an experience.

YOUR LIFE HAS BEEN THE BRIDGE, but you pass over it to a greater life. The bridges you build within the world are your organizations and your communities, which allow you to function in the world constructively and not chaotically. You are able to understand these bridges, yet the bridge from the world to the beyond will always be profoundly mysterious, for the beyond is always further than you have gone. Thus, you will have certainty and mystery all together.

THERE ARE A GREAT MANY ATTRACTIONS in the world that wish to be known as relationship. Indeed, they are not real relationship, for they are without purpose. In fact, they obstruct purpose. These attractions may be quite powerful because they appear to possess certain qualities that the individuals involved feel they are personally lacking. If these relationships were seen in truth, they would be seen to lack substance, for the motivating force behind them is need and uncertainty, rather than purpose. In order for these relationships to be sustained, the need and uncertainty that are their source must be maintained, for when the need and uncertainty are gone, so goes the relationship.

THE ROLE OF THE TEACHER is to broaden the student's realm of relationship. This is the path to God, for God is total relationship, relationship without limit. This experience of God cannot be maintained in the physical body for long periods, for it would render you incapable of functioning here in your daily activities. And yet if it can be touched upon, even briefly, it will enrich all of your activities and give you a perspective that is required for successfully living here.

YOUR RELATIONSHIP WITH THE TEACHERS is a doorway. It is not the end. It is not even the goal. It is the means. Yet it is not the total means, for the Teachers do not wish for you to rely upon them for everything. They must teach you to be reliant upon your own Knowledge. Thus, they restore to you what is yours without losing anything of themselves, thereby demonstrating the great fact that your relationships are restorative if they are seen correctly.

YOUR EXPERIENCE OF THE TEACHERS is an opportunity to experience relationship directly. It does not require the physical presence of the Teachers. Indeed, you all have physical presences and you rarely experience one another.

THE TEACHERS ARE INVISIBLE TO YOU. They will bear a physical resemblance only to accomplish a specific goal, and this will be rare indeed.

YOUR TEACHERS PRESENT THEMSELVES TO YOU without cloak, without subterfuge, without appearances. They must be felt. This is what we mean when we speak of the Presence. This is the purpose of this Teaching. For once this begins, then you will begin to remember your ancient relationships. When you remember your ancient relationships, the memory of your accomplishments will return to you, and the vast resources that you bring with you will begin to be recovered. Then your purpose in life will become evident.

NOW MANY OF YOU WILL PERHAPS ASK, "What is my purpose?" and we will respond again and again by offering you the means for regaining it. Is your purpose a definition? Is it merely a job in the world? Of course not. It is an experience that has grown to proportions great enough that you can share it with others.

THIS TEACHING IS MERELY A VEHICLE, like many others. Yet it is unique in some respects, for it introduces an ancient idea that has been long forgotten. Indeed, the idea of Spiritual Family has been barely mentioned in recorded history. It was forgotten.

AS THE WORLD BEGINS NOW to end the era of tribalism, struggling for unity in every corner of the world, the idea of Spiritual Families can now be taught and realized. It is the spiritual foundation for experiencing the world as part of a Greater Community of worlds.

AS YOUR WORLD ITSELF HAS A TRADITION of spiritual teachers and heroes, so the Greater Community has a spiritual tradition. Think of your religions. They are for humans only, are they not? They do not account for intelligent life elsewhere. They are prescriptions for humans. And yet there are prescriptions for all intelligent life, for nothing is excluded from the Greater Plan. It is within this context that the Spiritual Family has relevancy and can be experienced.

WE CANNOT ASK YOU TO LEARN greater Knowledge if your own personal life is in a state of catastrophe. Therefore, the first and most fundamental activity is setting your affairs in accordance with your Knowledge. Until this is accomplished, you will be struggling with your own self-conflict and demonstrating your self-conflict in your relationships with other people.

IT WILL TAKE TIME TO UNDERSTAND the nature of authority that exists between Teacher and student. Who is in charge? Whose will is being expressed? Whose desires are being fulfilled? And so forth. Only experience will demonstrate the beneficence of your Teachers in this regard. Only experience will demonstrate that the result is the reclamation of your Knowledge and all relationships that enhance and demonstrate Knowledge.

YOU ARE NOT NEEDED where everything is wonderful. You are needed where everything is not wonderful. When this life is over, everything can be wonderful. You went to great pains to come into this world, to be where things are not wonderful. In this world, things are not wonderful. Do you understand? Do not lie about this, or you shall reach the epitome of ignorance. You know things are not wonderful.

FIND OUT WHAT YOU ARE TO DO IN YOUR LIFE. That will resolve your relationships with everybody. You are out of accord with yourself.

DO YOU SEE? YOU MUST MAKE DECISIONS IN LIFE. You cannot have everything. If you attempt to have everything, you will not have anything.

SPIRITUAL ADVANCEMENT IN ALL PLACES is founded upon two premises. Regardless of the tradition or the teachers, the history or the customs, it is founded upon Knowledge in the world and Knowledge beyond.

IF YOU SEEK TO CULTIVATE KNOWLEDGE, you will not be able to determine the content of your Knowledge, for it will determine you, and as it grows, you will feel almost helpless in its Presence. And yet its Presence will be the comfort that you have always sought in all of your relationships, aspirations and endeavors.

SECRETS OF HEAVEN

THE EVENTS OF THE GREATER COMMUNITY in this sector have largely ignored your world. Your world is not even well known within this sector. However, time must bring change and growth. As the adolescent reaches adulthood, he or she must face life out in the world. So must your world face its adulthood with life in the Greater Community. This is a difficult transition, indeed, for your philosophy—indeed, the very ground of understanding upon which you live—understandably is associated with a human identity. It will not be easy to receive those who do not share this human identity. You will be as strange to them as they are to you.

THE TEACHERS TEACH EVERYWHERE, but they must teach their own kind.

DO NOT ATTEMPT TO REACH THE HIGHEST POINT, or you will miss the step that is in front of you, the step that has been awaiting you for so long.

YOU HAVE TWO POSSIBILITIES IN RELATIONSHIP ALWAYS. They will both lead to the same point if understood. You seek relationship to understand fantasy. And you seek relationship to develop Knowledge. There are no other possibilities, regardless of the attraction.

YOU CANNOT APPRECIATE KNOWLEDGE until you have tasted fantasy. This is true. But your appetite for fantasy cannot exceed your life force or capability. If so, you will destroy this opportunity to learn. You will end your life with nothing and will return again to try once more.

YOU MAY CHANGE YOUR CAREERS as often as you like, but nothing has changed except circumstances. Circumstances cannot satisfy a deeper inclination. If you have the deeper inclination, you must seek Knowledge, for that addresses the problem head-on. Then a career change will be brought through a series of steps. It is inevitable. You cannot develop Knowledge without constructive action; it is not possible. And you cannot have constructive action without Knowledge.

The Greater Community is a community of worlds. Yet the Greater Religion, if we may call it that, is established to serve beyond the traditions of individual worlds, for that is the realm of greater Knowledge. The Plan of God is not a Plan only for Christians or Buddhists or Muslims. It is a Plan for humans and non-humans. Within this context, your world's religions can have a new meaning and receive a new appreciation.

YOU ARE TO BE DISCOVERED, MY CHILDREN, by forces that you have never encountered in this life. If you are to understand them, it must be from Knowledge, not human speculation. If you are to foresee them and understand their intent, it must be from Knowledge. We have established this Teaching for this one purpose—to bring people into contact with Greater Community Spirituality and to provide a maximal opportunity to experience Knowledge, particularly at this time.

IN THIS PERIOD OF TIME, because you all sense imminent change, you react according to your personal inclinations. Some seek to revitalize old traditions and to establish old roots, while others seek to break all traditions and roots. Some attempt to reach God and escape being in the world, while others fall into despair. These are but different responses to the same basic feeling.

SOME ARE CALLED INTO SERVICE whether they are ready or not. If a building were on fire, you would respond whether you were ready or not. Would you sit and think, "Am I ready to have a fire in my life?"

WHEN YOU ARE COMPLETE IN THIS WORLD, Knowledge will be your main concern. When we speak of Knowledge, we do not speak of a body of information. We speak of a capacity for greater experience.

YOUR GREAT SPIRITUAL TEACHERS have unleashed untold violence upon the world, have they not? Those who took a public stance, could they guarantee a peaceful process? Certainly not. Yet their intent was not violent. You may seek to bring about change, but you will bring about combustion, violence, friction and confusion. It is unfortunate, but this is how people grow.

FOR THIS WORLD TO BECOME UNIFIED as one nation will involve untold violence, and yet it is a prospect that many cherish. Indeed, it is not only a cherished prospect, it is a necessity. Exposure to the Greater Community will bring this about. You cannot be at variance within your world and successfully encounter forces from beyond.

KNOWLEDGE YOU ALREADY HAVE, at least as far as it has been developed. To reclaim this is your first responsibility. To reclaim this, you must make a place for it. If your mind is totally filled with ideas, and you assume that this is adequate to cope with the physical and non-physical universe, then there is no space for Knowledge.

IF YOU WISH TO EXPERIENCE THE TEACHERS OF GOD who surround you, call them Angels or whatever you wish, you must have a place within yourself that is open for this. Therefore, empty your mind of grand thoughts. Then you may enter the present, which is the beginning of the experience of Knowledge.

A HIGH IDEAL GIVES DIRECTION to the conscious mind to seek its own depth. Yet it cannot take you into the depth. It is here that your Teachers, who are members of your Spiritual Family, will take a more direct role in your development. For from this place forward, you cannot lead yourself. You cannot go alone. You need guidance and companionship, a spiritual community both here and abroad.

THE ONE WHO THINKS he or she can enter Knowledge alone will risk insanity and despair. It is highly unwarranted.

FOR SOME, THE REALIZATION OF KNOWLEDGE is devastating in that it discounts so many of their personal beliefs. Knowledge may not appear to be like God at all. It is sober. It is clear. It does not take positions. It directs actions on its own accord without any reference to outside influences.

WE SPEAK OF THE GREATER COMMUNITY to stimulate Knowledge only, though it is unlikely that any of you will use it for this purpose.

WE ARE BOUND TO THE PHYSICAL by our obligations and desire to serve, which are the same. We have access to a Greater Reality, yet we exist here. We are nourished by this Greater Reality, and that is why we can exist in our capacity without misery. We serve our Spiritual Family, whom we love. We know our limits. We take full advantage of our strengths. We follow our Teachers, whom you cannot hear. We represent them as they represent those beyond them.

OUR TEACHINGS ARE LARGELY SECRET because of the possible conflict with existing traditions. Our primary service is the reclamation of Knowledge.

FOR SOME, THE TEACHERS WILL ALWAYS REMAIN in the background. As a result, they think their greater inspiration comes from themselves alone. Yet others cannot progress without conscious help. This is determined by the level of the individual and the mission they are to accomplish.

SECRETS
OF
HEAVEN

IT WOULD BE ACCURATE TO SAY that all Knowledge is the permanent establishment of relationship. Yet because your viewpoint regarding relationships is so transitory, this alone would not be sufficient to have a practical approach.

YOUR HISTORY must be an accumulation of gratitude, if it be real at all.

BELIEF SYSTEMS ARE ONLY TEMPORARY EXPEDIENCIES at best. They simply orient you toward your next step, and once this step is taken, they are largely set aside. Thus, if you are a Christian and through your spiritual practice you reach a greater association or body of Knowledge, you will be a good Christian no more and are likely to be thought of as a heretic. Now you are a good something else that no one can describe.

WHEN YOU ARE SPEAKING WITH KNOWLEDGE, you will have very little awareness of yourself. And yet you will be highly aware of what is around you.

ALL THIS SELF-GROWTH, what can it do for you? You either have Knowledge or you do not.

IF YOU DESTROY YOUR LIMITATIONS, you destroy the system of balance that keeps you progressing in a hopefully constructive manner. There are corrections to make along the way. Yet beyond this, do not tamper with your self-maintenance. People who do this go crazy.

YOU ARE MUCH TOO CONCERNED with your own progress, yet you have no reference to determine how well you are doing. Some people who are doing terribly are on the brink of a great discovery. Others who feel they are accomplishing great strides are merely stimulating themselves. How can you tell?

INNER GUIDANCE IS SIMPLY THE RE-ESTABLISHMENT of an established relationship. This is its true meaning. Though it seems remarkable to the one who receives it, it is simply a re-establishment of an old bond, as if an old friend has re-entered your life for a specific purpose.

KNOWLEDGE IS FAR MORE POWERFUL than you are personally. Therefore, you must prepare a place within your mind for Knowledge to emerge. It is not a plaything. Once its emergence has begun, it must continue.

YOU CANNOT ARGUE WITH WHAT YOU KNOW. You cannot bargain with what you know. Therefore, do not undertake the path of Knowledge unless you can accept its responsibilities.

BECAUSE THE TEACHERS ARE LARGELY INVISIBLE, it is difficult to project your images upon them. This allows a pure experience in relationship, for no relationship can be seen. Two bodies together is not a relationship. A relationship is not seen; it is experienced. A marriage cannot be seen; it is an understanding.

IT IS ILL ADVISED for you to seek greater spiritual experiences if your personal life in the world is in disarray. This will lead to dishonesty and ultimately failure.

IT IS, OF COURSE, UNDERSTOOD that beginning students will always attempt to use Knowledge to get more of what they want. This is understood. And yet it does not work very well, for Knowledge has its own purpose and its own expression. It is God within you. Yet it is God with a specific Plan.

WHEN THE KNOWN BECOMES STRONG, then you can participate in a greater reality beyond your personal interests, which is a practical form of salvation in this world.

SECRETS
OF
HEAVEN

THERE IS ALWAYS A GREAT DEAL OF DIFFICULTY with personal authority. Some cannot tolerate the idea of receiving a greater authority, and some will never claim their own. Yet all true teaching from beyond is to develop the individual to be self-motivating, to represent the truth of their own Knowledge.

THE BASIS FOR TRUE RELATIONSHIP is established at a deeper level, where even two dissimilar people find a basis for participation that cannot be destroyed by their divergent personalities.

JUST AS LITTLE CHILDREN cannot raise themselves, you cannot raise yourself. We could not raise ourselves. The return to God is the return to shared identity. Here there is a great learning responsibility that the individual must assume. This is certainly a challenge in and of itself.

YOU ARE ENTIRELY DEPENDENT upon God's Creation to accomplish anything of value. This is reason for gratitude in and of itself.

CHANGE IS INTRINSIC in a developmental process. Change does not produce peace. It produces friction. Peace is only possible in a steady state, which is undesired here. When a steady state has been established, then peace will reign. For when a steady state is reached, then there is no need to be in form. And since the idea of being formless is so unpopular here, obviously the world is in a state of development, change, growth, breakdown and rebuilding. It cannot be stopped.

YOUR WORLD IS ATTEMPTING TO UNIFY ITSELF into one community. It is a time of great discord. All worlds must go through this, just as all individuals must at some point become adults. They are parts of greater communities; they are not merely self-fulfilling individuals.

THERE IS NO POWER IN BEING AN INDIVIDUAL. It is a powerless state, for its basis cannot be rejuvenated. You are rejuvenated constantly because you are part of something greater that feeds you.

PEOPLE WANT PURPOSE, but not Knowledge. Do you see? They just say, "Tell me what to do so I'll feel better."

PEOPLE'S PERSONAL PROBLEMS ARE VERY SIMPLE if they are approached through Knowledge. People do not want to know, and yet they want to decide, and so it all becomes very difficult.

OFTEN CHANGE EXTERNALLY IS NOT THE ISSUE AT ALL. It is not addressing your need. The critical problem is that you do not know what you are doing, so you cannot do what you know.

THE INDIVIDUALS IN THIS WORLD who have successfully reclaimed Knowledge have had to escape convention to a very great degree because Knowledge is not conventional in any sense. And yet though they may appear erratic at times, their actions are always uniform and serve one purpose.

APPRECIATE YOUR LIMITATIONS and do not attempt to destroy them, or you will have no vehicle of service here.

YOU MUST SUCCESSFULLY NEGOTIATE THIS WORLD and use your physical abilities. You see, the Plan calls for the use of all your self-created abilities for a greater purpose. That is how everything is brought back into wholeness.

KNOWLEDGE WILL TAKE YOU BEYOND ALL CONCEPTS, for it is not based upon concepts. It is the reasoning faculty that is inherent within your true Self. It can negotiate the world far more effectively than you can, for it has only one purpose and not conflicting ones. A man or woman of Knowledge is a powerful force in the world.

IT IS IMPORTANT TO LOOK AT PRACTICAL ISSUES in a very fundamental way. Is it "yes" or "no"? It is not right or wrong; it is "yes" or "no". There is a great difference.

TO BE DISCERNING, YOU MUST BE HONEST, consistent, willing and appreciative of yourself and your possibilities. You must be patient and tolerant. These are very fundamental qualities. Here you find out what you want to know and what you don't want to know, what you are willing to resolve and what you are not.

SECRETS OF HEAVEN

KNOWLEDGE POSSESSES THE ACCOUNT of what must be done in life, and there must be an opportunity to express this, or it is not wise to discover it.

IF YOU WISH TO DISCOVER A GREATER TRUTH within yourself, you must have the available energy to participate. Knowledge is a very powerful force. It is the most powerful force. If you begin to gain access to it, you must have the strength and capacity to experience it and use it wisely. You must be very strong. You must be stable. Instability becomes dangerous, truly, when a greater capacity is being discovered. Therefore, the first step is to provide stability. Then a constructive change can occur with a minimum of risk.

THE SECOND STEP IS THE RECOGNITION and the acceptance that the power of discernment and decision making exists within you. As this becomes constructively employed with a minimum of idealism, it becomes an effective force in your life. Finally, you have a real basis for decision making that is sound and reliable.

THE THIRD STEP IS THE GREAT RECALL of Ancient Wisdom that you possess. All that you have acquired since time began is pooled in the wellspring of your Knowledge, including all the relationships of true value that you have established. These have not been forgotten. They are a part of you.

THE FOURTH STEP IS THE INTEGRATION of Knowledge into your daily affairs. This is an entirely natural process, for it is natural for you to do this. Once Knowledge is substantially integrated, it begins to provide direction. The Teachers are here to help you cultivate this.

LET US SPEAK FOR A MOMENT of the practical aspects of this achievement. As Knowledge becomes the dominant force in your awareness, it becomes impossible to make a mistake. Of course, this impossibility is dependent upon a very developed state. It will become more difficult to make mistakes, for you will feel a natural restraint that has become so strong that it cannot be ignored. Here you will be able to discern the relationship involvements that are truly beneficial. Your career, likewise, will be established on a sound foundation. You will be working where you know you need to be. That is the criterion. This requires faith only insofar as it does not point to the future, but provides certainty in the present. If faith is needed, you may be assured that certainty in the present will provide certainty in the future. Since you can only be in the present, certainty in the present is all that is needed.

BECAUSE HUMAN BEINGS are so incredibly fascinated with themselves, it is difficult for them to account for anything else.

IF YOU WERE TO GATHER INTO YOUR VISUAL VIEW members of your own Spiritual Heritage, they would represent quite an assortment of characters in many different forms, yet you would feel towards them like you would your own child, your dearest friend, your greatest comrade. This is Knowledge without limitation. It is not concerned with the form of things. It is concerned with the correctness and the content of things.

YOU DO NOT HAVE APPRECIATION FOR YOURSELF at this time, for you know you are not doing what is necessary. How can you appreciate the Teachers? They are not gods, you know. Do not worship them, for they will not allow this. But when you appreciate your accomplishments, you will know that you did not achieve them alone, and then your relationships can be experienced.

KNOWLEDGE DOES NOT PROVIDE CHOICES. Anyone who is in a state of Knowledge does not need to entertain choices. You have not yet gained Knowledge in this respect. That is why you entertain choices endlessly. It is wiser to develop Knowledge rather than to entertain more choices. When the truth is apparent, you will know what to do and you will undertake it at any cost. Indeed, it will not matter how long it takes to do it. It will draw upon all that you have achieved thus far and will call forth new strengths and experiences. So we are always back to the question of Knowledge.

MOST PEOPLE ARE NOT PATIENT ENOUGH to develop Knowledge. Everyone wants quick, easy resolutions that provide no foundation whatsoever. People change from one job to another and nothing has changed. They are as restless and irritated as always. It is a hopeless waste of youth.

WE DO NOT SPEAK OF RELINQUISHMENT in terms of material goods. We speak of relinquishment in terms of ideas that are not based upon what you know. They are merely aspirations that were established because you were lacking something else. People are afraid of Knowledge because they think it will rob them of their own certainty. Yet it provides the only real basis for certainty.

YOUR JOURNEY MAY BE DIFFICULT, but it is not without humor and happiness. Be in the middle, right where you are. Do not seek mastery. Seeking mastery will destroy you. Be where you are. Your Knowledge does not request more than that. Great spiritual ideals, lofty ambitions, great experiences of the light—this is not where people are. This is not Knowledge. Knowledge is at peace in the recognition of where it stands now. This is a practical experience of wholeheartedness and stability, of protection and purpose.

MANY OF YOU HAVE HAD EXPERIENCES of unequivocal Knowledge in the face of a great trial. This is an aspect of the great Power we speak of, except that we wish to cultivate it in the face of more peaceful circumstances.

THERE ARE STUDENTS IN DIFFERENT WORLDS. We teach students here to remember their heritage elsewhere, as we teach those elsewhere to remember their heritage here. Why do we do this? Because it is essential that these individuals become fully integrated and reclaim all aspects of their true identity and past accomplishments. This must be done entirely without fantasy.

STUDENTS HAVE STRANGE IDEAS about the Teachers. Therefore, often it is better that the Teachers remain unknown until such time that the student is well enough matured to use this awareness productively.

MANY PEOPLE ACKNOWLEDGE THE PRESENCE of the Teachers to some degree, but they have not entered the relationship yet, the actual relationship that they have with the Teachers. Relationship is dependent upon participation in the world. In shared participation, like a marriage or a great friendship, you must do something together.

THE TEACHERS HAVE A VERY DIFFICULT JOB, very difficult. That is why they have so few students. They must contribute to a very insane situation and set of circumstances. They must do this single-mindedly, with great patience and compassion. They must allow their beloved students to create calamity after calamity. They do not promote this, yet if that is the students' ambition, who can prevent them? Therefore, we discourage things that are obviously detrimental, yet we do not control or manipulate our students. That is not our function. Our true ability and resources are only waiting for others to call upon them. For this, we may have to wait a long time, a very long time.

THERE IS A GREATER RELIGIOUS TRADITION that serves the Greater Community. The Greater Community represents life on a larger scale of which your world is but a small part. The Plan of God serves all intelligent life. It is not the exclusive right of this little world. Therefore, for you to appreciate the Greater Plan, you must not have such a limited concept of who you are and what you have been. If you are to serve in the physical world, you must know what you have been in this life and to some extent in others. This must be accessed through Knowledge; otherwise, it is entirely useless. It must come through realization. If you think you were a great personage in a previous life, this has no value whatsoever except to inflate your sense of self-importance a little more. This is not what we speak of, please understand. We speak of the direct realization that who you are includes a greater body of life.

THOSE OF YOU WHO HAVE TRIED TO FOLLOW the religious traditions of this world with no success, why is this? Is it because these traditions are corrupt or fallible? No, that is not the reason. It is because they only reach a certain part of you. They do not reach your complete self. They do not cleanse all of you. You cannot wholeheartedly give yourself to them. They are incomplete for you. This is because you have emerged out of a greater religious tradition. This is the tradition that you have worked in for many, many years. Therefore, the reclamation of this tradition is essential for the development of your spiritual life. It may be difficult to accept this at first, for it seems that you are dabbling in fantastic things. Yet the truth is that you are seeking for your religious tradition. If you cannot find it in the traditions of the world, you had better look elsewhere, for this world does not represent the religious traditions of the entire galaxy.

FOR THOSE WHO HAVE UNDERTAKEN their progress primarily in this world, there are traditions here that are satisfactory to their needs. Yet this does not account for everyone. Therefore, the Teachers who represent Greater Community Spirituality seek those students who need this tradition. Without finding this tradition, they will be estranged in this world, always feeling homeless, always blaming the world and other people for their estrangement, always seeking fulfillment in personal relationships and failing.

YOU NEED A LARGER PERSPECTIVE to comprehend the work of God. God is not human. God does not think like a human. God is not made in your image. God has no image. The Source of all life accounts for all life.

IF YOU ARE TO UNDERSTAND AND APPRECIATE the nature of those whom God has sent to help you, then in time you will begin to share their perspective and see what evolution means on a larger scale. Then you will begin to understand your duties and know what growth means here on Earth.

IF YOU WISH TO SERVE A GREATER PURPOSE and to experience a Greater Source, then you must learn what this means. You cannot define the way. People attempt perfection because they are convinced of error, but they do not know perfection. You cannot know perfection from error. You can only know error. Perfection is not erasing error. It is gaining wisdom, compassion, ability, capacity and love.

If you could see evolution on a larger scale, you would most certainly adjust your expectations of yourself. Those few individuals who attain seeming perfection find themselves at a new beginning upon leaving this life, yet they need not be here any longer. Now, instead of transcending their humanity, they must learn to encounter the identities of the universe.

PEOPLE OFTEN ASK, "WHY DO I NEED TEACHERS?" The answer is very simple. It is because you do not know anything. You believe that by perfecting your personality or body that you will attain great heights. Yet we assure you, you will attain great frustration. A perfect personality may have no more Knowledge than an imperfect one. Though there are adjustments to make in your behavior and thinking, of course, perfecting your behavior to meet your standards is not the Path of Knowledge. Knowledge is not ideas. It is experience. It is relationship. It is God.

WE PRESENT THIS IDEA OF THE GREATER RELIGION. Why is it greater? Greater does not mean better. It is only greater because it accounts for a larger reality.

HUMAN BEINGS ARE NOT SENT HERE to achieve ultimate reality. That is not your purpose. Your purpose in being here is to complete being here.

It is true that Knowledge must be gained through experience. An intellectual pursuit it is not. Your intellect was not created to comprehend the universe. It was created to negotiate the particulars of your physical life, at which it has become fairly sophisticated. Yet it cannot appreciate what is felt and what is known. Therefore, do not use your intellect inappropriately. It has its true application, and a useful one at that.

OUR WORK, THEN, IS RELIGIOUS IN NATURE because it deals with God. It deals with a greater life. In this world, you cannot approach the greatest life; you can only approach a greater life. You must go through the stages of evolution. Understanding this, you will be able to recognize what needs to be done, what can be done and what cannot be done. You will see your true involvement and your true requirements, without placing impossible burdens upon your shoulders.

To be alone in this world is a terrible destiny. Yet you are not alone. Before you came into this world, you were not alone and those who were with you then are with you now. To regain this memory is to regain consciousness of life in the visible and of life beyond. Then the barriers of illusion begin to fall away. Then you can begin to comprehend the Presence rather than feel it only.

RELIGIOUS EXPERIENCE EVOLVES and necessitates a growing point of view.

YOU CAN ALWAYS DOUBT WHAT WE SAY. But it is more difficult to doubt what you know. Whatever our engagement is through time, the only real result will be what you know.

WE HAVE TOLD A NUMBER OF PEOPLE WHAT TO DO. They have had mixed reactions. Some felt that their personal feelings were extremely violated. They were affronted by our advice, which they had earnestly sought. Yet their personal affront was not a reflection on us. It was simply that they were afraid or feeling incapable of undertaking what we had indicated.

THE HOLY SPIRIT is actually the activating agent of Knowledge. It is the communication of God to awaken.

THE PURPOSE OF THIS IS KNOWLEDGE. There is no one to idolize. There are no heroes here. We remain invisible. You cannot worship us. In time, you will understand the wisdom of this and why it is so essential in order for us to be effective. Even the great ones in your world who have gone so far, who contributed their Knowledge, did not seek to become idols of worship. It is their Knowledge that has been neglected, for people are afraid of Knowledge, yet Knowledge is the purpose.

IF YOU YEARN FOR IT, SEEK IT. You cannot define it. You cannot predict the outcome, but you seek Knowledge because it is natural for you to do so. For Knowledge contains the memory of your Creator, of your help and of your meaning in this world.

NASI NOVARE CORAM

The Engagement

THE ENGAGEMENT

As revealed to
Marshall Vian Summers
on April 16, 2011
in Boulder, Colorado

The Higher Authority is speaking to you now,
Speaking through the Angelic Presence,
Speaking to a part of you that is the very center and
Source of your Being,
Speaking beyond your social conditioning,
Beyond your ideas and beliefs
And the ideas and beliefs of your culture and even your religion.

The Higher Authority has a Message for the world
And for each person in the world.
The Message is more than an idea.
It is more than even a set of ideas.
It is a calling and a confirmation,
Calling you to respond and
Confirming that there is a deeper nature within you
And within all the people of the world.
The confirmation is a turning point in your ability to respond.

The Power and the Presence preside over the physical universe,
A universe far greater and more expansive
Than what you can possibly imagine and
Even beyond the physical universe
To the greater realms of Creation itself,

Which is something that few people in the world
Have even considered to be possible.

Yet the Higher Authority speaks to you
In your most private place,
The center of your Being,
Deep beneath the surface of your mind.
This is your greatest relationship.
It is the source of meaning and purpose in all of your relationships
With people, with places and even with things.

You need this Higher Authority now
To speak to the deeper part of you,
To acquaint you with the deeper part of you and
To prepare you for living in a new world and
For engaging with a universe of intelligent life
That is the Greater Community of life.

You know not of these things,
But they are part of you.
Perhaps you have experienced your deeper nature
In times of clarity,
Times of prescience and
Times even of disappointment
When you were able to hear
Beyond your desires and your fears and
The desires and fears of others.

The Higher Authority is calling to you,
Calling to you down through the ancient corridors of your mind,
Calling to you beyond your beliefs and your preoccupations.

For God has spoken again

And the Word and the Sound are in the world.
It is a deeper communication,
Far deeper and more profound than the intellect can comprehend.

It speaks of a greater purpose and a deeper responsibility
And a greater association, both within this world and beyond.
Through this association
You become a bridge,
A bridge to the world,
A bridge to your Ancient Home,
From which you have come and
To which you will return.

People want many things.
They have great fears—
The fear of losing,
The fear of not having,
The fear of deprivation,
The fear of oppression,
The fear of pain and suffering
And pain of death.

But the Higher Authority speaks beyond all of these things.
It is the Creator speaking to Creation.
Creation within you is the deeper mind we call Knowledge.
It is the permanent part of you.
It is the part of you that existed before this life
And will exist after this life,
Journeying through the realms of Separation,
Guided only by the power of the Voice.

People want many things.
They have great fears.

Many people have firm beliefs.
But the Higher Authority speaks beyond these things
To all who can see and hear and
Who can respond at a deeper level.

You cannot evaluate this.
It is greater than your mind.
You cannot debate this, for it is beyond your capabilities.
It is mysterious because it is pervasive.
Its origin is beyond this world and all worlds,
So you cannot imagine it.

But the experience is so deep
That it can alter the course of your life
And awaken you from your dream of separation,
Calling you out of your preoccupations
And your associations
And everything
So that you may hear the Ancient Voice,
So ancient that it speaks of a life beyond your reckoning,
But a life that is your life.

God knows what is coming over the horizon.
God knows why you are here.
God has sent you here for a purpose.
Your plans and goals rarely account for this.
It is something greater.
It is something more simple and less grandiose.
It is something essential to your Being
And to your nature and to your design.
It is the most primary relationship you have,
The deepest love,
The greatest affinity.

It unites you with yourself and
Brings your life into focus.

It calls you out of situations
That are harmful or that have no promise for you,
Calls you into a greater participation in the world,
Guided by the mysterious Ancient Voice,
A Voice unlike anything you have ever heard,
Deeper than anything you have ever felt,
Greater than anything you can see or touch.

People want many things.
They are driven by great fear.
Even their pleasures are full of fear and apprehension.
But the Ancient Voice is beyond fear,
And when you respond, you are beyond fear.

Who can say what this is?
Who can evaluate this?
Do not be stupid and think in terms of productivity.
Do not be analytical.
For this is happening at a deeper and more profound level.
Do not shrink from this,
For this is your life, your purpose and your calling.

The Presence and the Grace are with you,
But you are looking at other things.
Your mind is elsewhere.
That which redeems you and restores you
Is with you now,
But you are looking in the other direction.

The Revelation is in the world.
God has come again
With a greater Message for humanity
And a preparation for a difficult and
Hazardous future for the human family.

What is this?
What does it mean?
Why is it happening?
How do you prepare?

Only the Revelation can answer these questions.
Setting yourself apart you cannot answer these questions.

People want many things.
They are very distracted.
They are very preoccupied,
But they do not know where they are or what they are doing.
Their goals are the goals of society for the most part.
They do not know where they are going in life
Or why they are here
Or who sent them
And what will restore them
And fulfill them
And give their life purpose and direction.

The Ancient Voice is speaking to you now.
You will hear the Ancient Voice responding within yourself,
For your connection is very deep.
It is like the rivers that run underground,
Under the desert,
Underground rivers of the purest water,
But which cannot be seen from the surface
And which cannot be found except by other means.

While you live your life at the surface,
Deep within you,
You are connected to the Divine.
And this connection is experienced
Through the calling and the response,
By following a deeper Voice and a greater direction.

People ask, Why? Why is this happening?
They must stop and listen
And learn to listen,
Bring their attention fully into this moment
So they can hear and feel and see
That the Revelation is stirring within them.
So the Revelation stirs,
The Revelation within each person.
This is how God speaks to the world
At the Time of Revelation.

This is relationship at the deepest and most significant level.
You cannot break away from God,
For God goes everywhere with you.
God is with you every moment,
In every activity that you do.
Only in your thoughts can you be separate,
Associating yourself with other things,
Identifying with other things.
But the Ancient Voice is within you,
Calling you to respond,
Guiding you,
Holding you back.

To understand your deeper premonitions
And the urgings of your heart,

You must begin to listen.
Listen within yourself.
Listen to the world without judgment and condemnation.
Listen for the signs of what is coming.
Listen to how you must respond.
Listen to who to be with and who not to be with.

Here you do not follow fear.
Here there is no condemnation.
Here there is a greater discernment
And a greater recognition.

God has put Knowledge within you
To guide you and to protect you
And to lead you to a greater life and
Participation in the world.
It resides beyond the realm and the reach of the intellect.
It is happening at a deeper level.

Once you begin to experience this,
You begin to gain a greater discernment.
You become careful about what you do
And who you associate with.
You listen deeply to others to see
If you should participate with them
And what they are communicating to you.

People believe many things,
But they know very little.
They are living at the surface of the mind,
Which is turbulent and chaotic
And governed by the winds
And the passions of the world.

Their beliefs are a substitute for the deeper relationships.
Their preoccupations are an avoidance of
The greater engagement they are destined to have.
Standing apart, they cannot see.
They cannot know.
They cannot respond.
They are dominated by their thoughts,
By their mind, by their reactions.
They are slaves, living slavishly.

But the Mystery is within them.
It is the most important thing in life.
Beyond achieving goals,
Securing wealth
And companionship
And recognition in society,
It is the most important thing
Because it is the arena of a greater engagement.

The Mystery is the source of everything important.
All the great inventions and contributions,
The great relationships,
The great experiences,
They all come from the Mystery—
Who you are,
Why you are here,
What is calling you,
Your greater association,
Your destiny with certain people in the world,
Your ability to find your way,
While everyone around you
Is sleeping, dreaming and unresponsive.

This is a journey you must take
Or your life will be a troubled dream
And no more.

When you return to your Spiritual Family
After you leave this world,
They will look at you to see
If you have accomplished your task,
If you made the deeper connection.
And you will know if you have
Or you have not.
There is no judgment and condemnation,
Only recognition here.
Here what was mysterious before becomes reality itself.
And your priorities are clear.
There are no distractions.
There is no resistance.

You will want to return,
Saying to yourself,
"This time I will remember.
I know now.
I can see now.
I will remember."
But you must remember while you are here.
That makes all the difference.
That is the beginning of everything important.
That is the turning point of your life.

It is only mysterious because you have been divorced from it,
Caught up in the world of form,
Lost in the world,
Growing up as an individual,

Adapting to a difficult, changing world.
Then something comes to remind you,
And you begin to feel that the Mystery is with you
And in you
And influencing you.

Its Source is beyond the physical reality,
For who you are is beyond the physical reality.
Where you are going ultimately is beyond the physical reality,
But you are meant to be here,
For you have been sent here for a purpose.
That is the Mystery.

We speak of these things
To engage you at a deeper level,
To call forth that which is authentic,
To speak to a part of you
You barely know,
Which is the greater part of you.
This part of you will respond
Because of our ancient commitment together.

You are afraid of this,
But you desire it at the same time.
It is a natural desire,
More natural than anything else you are doing
Or could do in the world.

It is the Engagement.

ABOUT MARSHALL VIAN SUMMERS

In 1983, a man named Marshall Vian Summers left his home, his work and the city in which he lived to wander in the desert, responding to the call and beckoning of a mysterious inner voice.

His inexplicable relationship with this mysterious voice began some eight years earlier. Working as a teacher for the blind and the visually impaired, Marshall began to receive profound guidance on how to best serve his students and call forth their deeper abilities. This grew into a powerful inner voice experience, which slowly began to guide him towards people and situations to which he was called.

As time went on, Marshall left his work as a teacher of the blind to become a teacher of self-knowledge and inner guidance, which he did for a number of years.

Then one night, a shocking encounter occurred which changed everything. After eight years, Marshall came into full contact with the source of this Voice that had been guiding him all along.

It was following this shattering experience that the Source of his guidance instructed him, without explanation, to leave his teaching and his students and to depart all that he had worked to build.

Without understanding why, Marshall followed this inexplicable request. He departed the people, place and work in which he was engaged and began a period of wandering, unsure of what the Voice would ask of him next.

In time, his wandering brought him to the deserts of the American Southwest. Arriving there, he found a place of retreat and stayed there for a time. It was during his retreat, on a cold, quiet night, that the Voice came to him again and instructed him to "record." He was directed to return to the city, and once there, to begin receiving a series of teachings.

Marshall opened himself to the Voice more fully now, and the Voice spoke through him. Words led to sentences, sentences led to chapters and ultimately to entire books. Marshall's understanding of the mysterious Voice of Revelation grew over time as the scope and power of the Revelation unfolded before him. What began as a small stream of guidance given to one man would become a rushing river of Revelation for people around the world.

Three decades after that cold, quiet night in the desert, a vast spoken Revelation has ensued. What started as teachings emerging from a deep and mysterious voice has grown to be a Revelation over 9000 pages in scope, given in over 20 volumes and across thousands of angelic encounters—all delivered from a vast Angelic Assembly, speaking together as one, through Marshall Vian Summers, their Messenger.

Over these three decades, the Voice spoke through this man, was audio recorded and then transcribed, maintaining its complete purity. The Voice that spoke to him can now be heard by people everywhere, allowing them to have their own experience of its power, wisdom and authenticity. The actual Voice of Revelation can now be heard for the first time. This is a New Message from God reaching the people directly in its original form.

Secrets of Heaven contains the mysterious words and phrases originally spoken in the earliest days of the Revelation. These are the first gifts, arising from the depths of mystery, to touch the hearts and minds of humanity today.

A New Message from God has been given. It speaks down the Ancient Corridors of the mind, speaking to the Heart of Creation in all who can respond.

DEEPER INTO THE MYSTERY

GO DEEPER INTO THE MYSTERY that surrounds your presence in the world. Hear the spoken revelation of the New Message from God, which can reveal to you your greater purpose and destiny in life.

The Voice of Revelation

available on CD or online:

The Initiation

www.newmessage.org/initiation

The Night Meditation

www.newmessage.org/nightmeditation

Spiritual Fire

www.newmessage.org/spiritualfire

The Rays of Initiation

www.newmessage.org/rays

The Engagement

www.newmessage.org/engagement

To experience the growing library of spoken revelations, visit www.newmessage.org/experience

THE MOVEMENT GROWS

Secrets of Heaven is moving across the world. Part of a vast Revelation called the New Message from God, these secrets have the power to awaken the sleeping brilliance in people everywhere and bring new inspiration and wisdom to a world facing growing conflict and other dire challenges.

Now this gift from Heaven is being received worldwide. Translated into 16 languages and studied by people in 72 countries, the New Message is inspiring a movement of purpose, relationship and contribution across all boundaries of language, nationality and religion.

Learn more about events, teachings and free educational opportunities and meet others who are reading *Secrets of Heaven* and feeling the mysterious call to respond.

www.newmessage.org

Lightning Source UK Ltd.
Milton Keynes UK
UKOW04f1841290913

218165UK00001B/27/P